TABLE OF CONTENTS

I0453155

Book Cover by James Chakhtoura
ISBN# 979-8-9894451-0-3

OUR MISSION & VISION

Tilting The Balance™ is a transformative system designed to help individuals cultivate balance, purpose, and fulfillment in every area of life. The origin of this framework traces back to December 26th, 2019, when Justin experienced a moment of absolute clarity while sitting in his mother's driveway, just before leaving to visit his grandparents. Every hair on his body stood up as an undeniable realization hit him. Despite consuming countless personal and professional development books and content alongside his close friend Nicolas Houpt, they both remained stuck. Nothing seemed to be working to help them overcome their cycles of acquiring knowledge without attaining significant results. At that moment, Justin called Nick with a proposal:

"Nick! Let's commit to a thirty-day challenge together, hold each other accountable, and write a book about our experiences!" What if Nick would not have answered that call, in more ways than one? That single conversation sparked what they never could have initially imagined would evolve into what it became over the course of nearly six years.

Through rigorous testing, refinement, and real-world application over that time, Justin and Nick transformed their initial thirty-day experiment into a proven framework. What began as two friends trying to break free from their own limiting patterns and beliefs developed into a complete, practical methodology that has helped countless individuals create lasting transformation. In the process, they discovered something profound. Most people are not starving for more information. They are overwhelmed by it. Never in human history have people had more access to information. There are more books, podcasts, videos, courses, and educational streams of advice available than one person could spend an entire lifetime consuming. Yet individuals today struggle to apply what they learn more than ever before. How is this possible?

Around every corner are free newsletters, posts, or videos, accompanied by advertisements selling strategies to get rich quick, lose weight without effort, or instantaneously turn from failure to success. Even when programs are built with integrity, genuine does not always mean effective, and effective does not always mean comprehensive. A program can work within its narrow focus but still fail to help someone integrate that growth into the rest of their life. Think of life like a master puzzle where purpose forms the complete image, but within that larger picture are smaller, distinct sections representing relationships, health, career, finances, and other aspects of existence and personal growth. Most people try to work on these areas independently, treating each as an isolated challenge. Real progress is not about excelling in one area while neglecting others. *Tilting The Balance*™ reveals how all the scattered pieces from different areas of life fit together within the bigger picture of purpose. It is about knowing how to implement insights in balance so that each piece connects together and strengthens the whole. Growth in one area should support, rather than disrupt, the entirety of well-being.

This discovery revealed a critical gap in personal development. Despite years of consuming countless resources, Justin and Nick remained stuck because no method existed to teach them how to strategically apply everything they were learning. Born out of their mutual frustration, what makes *Tilting The Balance*™ unique is that it addresses this execution gap that many traditional resources overlook. While these tend to focus solely on either motivation, mindset, or teaching practical strategies on specific subjects, this framework provides what often remains the missing piece. It offers a clear methodology that helps individuals compartmentalize their thoughts, define their purpose, organize their priorities, and execute with precision, in that specific order.

By providing proven frameworks, built-in accountability with "*The 3-4-30 Challenge*SM," and comprehensive step-by-step guidance, paired with practical exercises and structured implementation strategies, individuals seeking meaningful change can finally gain the structure needed to turn knowledge into lasting results. This formulaic approach helps determine what to learn, why it matters, how it serves growth, when to learn it, where to best focus efforts, and who to learn from. Rather than mindlessly consuming content, it provides strategic clarity on exactly what knowledge is needed and how to implement it most effectively.

As the authors, our mission is to empower one billion people to believe in themselves, practice ongoing disciplined action, and live a complete life of love, passion, purpose, and fulfillment. We understand that reaching one billion people will likely extend far beyond our own lifetimes, and we welcome that challenge. Whether it takes generations or centuries, we envision *Tilting The Balance*™ outlasting us. We want it to become a foundational resource in both personal and professional development, the first guide that people turn to when they decide they are ready to transform their lives and circumstances.

Our objective is not about the number of individuals who directly read our material or engage with our programs. If we can influence one person to use this system to launch something that revolutionizes the world, one person to treat others more positively, or another to inspire growth in their community, then each of those leads to compounding contributions toward the billion lives we aim to reach. The more someone improves their relationship with themselves, the stronger family member, friend, partner, professional, and person they can become. The better someone treats others, the more compassion they may inspire in return. That influence extends far beyond people. It affects how we care for the planet, the animals and creatures we share it with, and the causes we choose to support. Each person carries responsibility to leave the world better than they found it.

This is how we measure our impact. It begins with each reader. With you. If this book creates a personal breakthrough, if you start a meaningful project, or if you change the lives of others because of what you learn here, please share it in any way possible. Tag us online, use our dedicated hashtag #TTB4E (Tilting The Balance For Everyone), or contact us directly at www.TiltingTheBalance.com/ContactUs to share your story.

What matters most to us is that transformation is happening. We see a world where people recognize their inherent value and use their gifts intentionally, without wasting their time, energy, resources, or opportunities. Too many people spend their lives without ever discovering their purpose or reaching their greatest potential. When you transform your own life and inspire others to do the same, every life improved becomes proof that our mission is alive and flourishing.

Thank you for being part of this community. We appreciate you and are beyond grateful for everyone who chooses to join us. The better we can all help people live, the better the world becomes for everyone.

Let us all work together to tilt the balance for the best today.

OUR COMMITMENT TO YOU

Humanity is meant for more than merely existing. Each person deserves to live with love, meaning, passion, and fulfillment while actualizing their full potential and making lasting contributions to the world.

We believe everyone possesses this ability, yet the majority remain held back by fear, confusion, overwhelm, procrastination, distraction, and self-doubt. This is precisely why we created this guide.

Within these pages, you will find no empty theories, vague ideas, or wishful thinking. Instead, you will discover proven concepts tested in the real world and drawn from practical experience, all designed to support immediate growth and progress. These same principles have enabled us and countless others to break free from limiting patterns, set intentional goals, and take meaningful action across all areas of life.

The following pages contain powerful techniques that can be implemented immediately to organize mental clutter, establish clear initiatives, and move decisively toward desired outcomes. This represents the foundation of a larger personal development formula we have built, with our ultimate mission being to positively impact at least one billion people worldwide.

Consider this material a starting point and invitation to something greater, as our dedication extends far beyond this content. Whether you continue through our complete *Tilting The Balance*™ system, connect with us directly at www. TiltingTheBalance.com, or apply these strategies independently, we remain committed to supporting your journey with the highest quality resources and empowering information to help you navigate challenges while continuing your growth.

As the authors, we thank you for choosing to invest in both yourself and us through this work. Our dreams cannot come true without yours doing the same.

- Justin M. Bullock & Nicolas A. Houpt

INTRODUCTION

The truth is, no book, course, or program can make a difference in your life unless you are willing to show up and put in the work. If you are ready to break free from past patterns, challenge the way you think, and commit to real, lasting growth, then what we are about to review ahead has the power to change everything.

If you do not start taking intentional action, if you do not apply what you are about to learn, and if you keep doing what you have always done, then the outcome is virtually inevitable: you will likely keep getting more of what you are currently getting. Nothing significant or noteworthy tends to change unless we do. We presume you picked up this book for a reason, and that something inside of you is in search of something greater.

Welcome to your first step into *Tilting The Balance*™, a research-backed system for living with clarity, purpose, and the ability to create a life rich with joy, meaning, and fulfillment.

As the authors, we created *Tilting The Balance*™ because we understand firsthand how challenging it feels to be out of control. Before developing this method, we struggled to overcome negative coping mechanisms, self-destructive habits, and specific addictions that kept us trapped in cycles we desperately wanted to break. The feelings of helplessness, shame, and frustration that come with being unable to alter the behaviors we know are harmful? Those are feelings we know quite intimately.

For many years prior to and even during the development of *Tilting The Balance*™, we were consuming a plethora of personal and professional books, podcasts, videos, seminars, or anything else we could find that would give us the answers we needed to change. The sheer amount of proposed solutions we learned about left us feeling overwhelmed, scattered, and without the structured support we needed to generate the results we wanted. What was missing from every other methodology we encountered was a clear understanding of how to compartmentalize life effectively and maintain real accountability. We needed something that could help us organize our thoughts, prioritize what mattered most to us, and execute a plan with comprehensive understanding of how to simultaneously evolve both our internal mindset and external actions.

Through the development and application of *Tilting The Balance*™, we were able to build that very formula. The success we experienced for ourselves and for those who began participating in our method along with us was so profound, our next steps became crystal clear. We knew we had to begin to share it on a mass scale. Our mission that emerged to help one billion people worldwide stems from a simple truth: *Tilting The Balance*™ makes meaningful growth so much easier to navigate, we believe it should become the common standard for personal transformation.

Central to this evolution is understanding the importance of discovering your individual why. Your why, your reason for being, functions as the emotional force behind every pivotal decision you make. This moves you forward when challenges arise, drives your motivation when things get difficult, and gives your goals and aspirations the deepest meaning. Without a solid why, feeling lost, overwhelmed, unmotivated, distracted; it becomes an all too common condition.

Most people struggle to uncover their authentic purpose because they remain unaware of what they truly want, or they lack the knowledge of how to pursue what they do want. Along with that, they doubt their abilities, or believe their dreams are impossible, causing them to never take meaningful action. These barriers keep countless individuals stuck in lives that feel empty, repetitive, or unfulfilling.

Consider the entrepreneur who spent decades in a corporate job before finally launching the business they had always yearned to build, the personal trainer who overcame years of poor health by committing to the necessary lifestyle changes and is now helping others do the same, or any of those who overcame personal adversity to make their desires a reality. In many of these cases, breakthroughs usually transpired not because these individuals learned some new, revelatory information, but rather because they began applying their existing knowledge by connecting it all with a compelling enough reason to take persistent action.

When someone can clearly define and articulate their purpose for being, everything shifts. A strong vision of personal success emerges, along with the resilience to keep pushing forward regardless of any challenges or obstacles that may appear. The exercises and techniques presented in the following pages are designed to guide you through the process of uncovering and strengthening your own foundational purpose.

Our next book in this series, *Tilting The Balance™: A Guided Workbook for Clarity, Purpose, and Transformation*, delivers our unique strategy for achieving this clarity in greater depth. The workbook demonstrates how to effectively compartmentalize and prioritize all areas of life using what we call "The 10 Categories of Life." This complete system helps organize your life strategically, prioritize what matters most, and establish actionable plans paired with ongoing accountability. We also provide a thorough account of how to evolve both internal and external directives along the way. Many personal growth philosophies emphasize either mindset or action, but real change happens when the two work harmoniously together. Our method goes beyond simply thinking differently by applying those mental shifts in practical, measurable ways.

While our workbook provides the entire comprehensive *Tilting The Balance™* framework complete with all "The 10 Categories of Life," the guide you have here contains all of the powerful, life-changing content you will need to drive immediate results. As its own standalone resource, the strategies you will learn here represent a more direct version of the proven techniques that can fundamentally shift how you approach personal growth. Through these teachings, you can expect to learn how to clarify your individual purpose and desires, challenge limiting beliefs, establish a mindset that empowers your endeavors, and develop concrete action plans that turn insights into measurable, lasting progress.

Most importantly, you will discover key content from our workbook, included in this guide, that has been designed to deliver the formula for meaningful results by clearing mental clutter and building early momentum. This includes our flagship program, *"The 3-4-30 Challenge℠,"* that serves as the foundation of our entire strategy by enforcing continuous accountability, combined with practices like "The Mind Dump" that generate immediate breakthroughs in organization and focus.

Additionally, you will learn our exclusive Vision Gazing^{SM} technique, which is also included in the workbook, an advanced method that elevates traditional visualization to extraordinary levels, ensuring every goal aligns perfectly with your deepest aspirations. You can also look forward to us covering long-term vision and direction building exercises, including how to develop a compelling Chief Aim Statement, riveting mission and vision statements, and motivational vision boards that serve as daily inspiration.

Lastly, we explore powerful mindset reinforcement techniques including visualization, affirmations, meditation, and gratitude practices, alongside proven implementation strategies such as how to go about establishing effective daily habits, creating personal boundaries, and mastering hard scheduling methods. These approaches work together to enhance focus and maintain unwavering consistency.

Together, we will cover how to manage your thoughts and emotions while establishing the right disciplines, structured practices, and daily activities proven to cultivate desired results. Too often, people find themselves distracted by memories and worries about the past, anticipation and concerns about the future, or lost in the constant noise of modern life. True change, however, can only begin in the present moment. Our framework demonstrates how to use the now to establish clarity, calmness, and control while combining mindfulness with structured goal-setting, habit reinforcement, and ongoing accountability, enabling sustainable progress in every chosen area of life.

By the time you conclude this read, the role of small, purposeful actions in creating lasting results will become clear, along with the significance of embracing progress over perfection throughout your journey. It is the smaller actions we take daily that shape our more substantial outcomes over time. No matter if your focus is on your health, relationships, finances, career, or any other important aspects of your life, mastering the art of balancing priorities and managing tasks remains the key to achieving lasting fulfillment.

As you move through this material, it is intentional that certain principles and strategies will appear more than once. Real growth comes not from reading something once but from reinforcement, repetition, and application. The more these ideas become ingrained into your subconscious mind, the more they can further enhance shaping your thoughts, feelings, daily actions, and long-term success.

Our entire philosophy also avoids perfectionism and quick fixes. Success emerges through constant awareness, appreciation of the present moment, and learning to love accepting personal responsibility. It requires thoughtful planning, consistent action, and faith in knowing that everything will always unfold favorably, even when we might make mistakes or when life may take unexpected turns. There is no way to force results and fulfillment other than doing the required work in the time it takes to become the person who believes in themselves and the actions they take. It is a process to adopt, implement, and reinforce this mentality.

Now that you know what to expect, we are excited to be part of your personal transformation. Whether this marks the first introduction to our method or you have already begun exploring the *Tilting The Balance*™ philosophy in some capacity, let this be a catalyst, compass, and reminder that almost anything is possible. As you continue from here, be cognizant of the fact that every decision, regardless of its size, holds the potential to either shape you closer to or further away from the life you envision most. That is why the best time to begin is right now. Life is far too precious to waste and way too short to live with regrets.

As you implement these strategies and begin experiencing real change, we genuinely want to hear about your progress! Your breakthrough moments, victories, and insights inspire us and help strengthen our mission to impact lives worldwide. As we committed in our opening, we remain dedicated to supporting your journey with the highest quality resources and empowering information to help you navigate challenges while continuing your growth. You can find all of the channels to connect with us and discover all of our current resources, programs, and support options to enhance your personal development journey at www. TiltingTheBalance.com.

Remember, personal development is not a destination but a continuous journey of becoming. Take the first step today, enjoy yourself along the way, and let your future self thank you for having the courage to begin.

CHAPTER 1:
THE POWER OF YOUR MINDSET

Your mindset is the collection of beliefs, attitudes, and assumptions that shape how you interpret and respond to everything that happens in your life. It serves as the mental lens through which you view yourself, others, and the world around you. This internal framework determines what you see as possible or impossible, what you consider to be opportunities or obstacles, and how you define circumstances, successes, or setbacks.

Developing a disciplined, controlled mindset extends far beyond positive thinking. It demands a critical shift in perspective that aligns perpetual thoughts with the results you aspire to create. The beliefs you hold have the ability to propel you forward or keep you stuck in place. This reality makes uncovering and reshaping limiting beliefs the essential first step toward genuine transformation.

When you learn to identify restrictive beliefs and cultivate empowering new viewpoints, you can accelerate progress and elevate your results. Where *Tilting The Balance™: A Guided Workbook for Clarity, Purpose, and Transformation* offers deeper strategies and techniques for permanently rewiring your subconscious mind for success, this resource provides the core insights needed to begin. This is why we start here with the first fundamental for reaching new heights. It all begins with your mental framework.

Personal beliefs are what tend to dictate the majority of our individual outcomes. They govern our thoughts, emotions, actions, and ultimately, our achievements. However, it remains essential to recognize that while mental approaches powerfully influence results, countless variables will always remain beyond our direct control. External circumstances, other people's choices and actions, economic conditions, and unexpected life events represent factors that no amount of positive thinking is completely capable of managing. What does remain controllable, however, is our perspective on everything that happens to us along with our responses to every situation.

To better dictate our futures, awareness of our current positions and of the next best courses of action must first be developed. Self-awareness represents the single most vital element in any transformative process. It requires total honesty and genuine willingness to confront both strengths and weaknesses in all areas where growth is necessary. It is vital to gain awareness of who, what, where, when, why, and how anything in our lives may need adjustment.

Following awareness comes the ability to claim complete responsibility for our lives. This does not mean we take the blame for everything that happens, but rather that we learn to accept full ownership when we have a part in a situation. Real breakthroughs happen when attention shifts from reactivity to proactivity. As we stated, life has an uncanny way of presenting challenges, obstacles, setbacks, and unexpected turns that will be completely outside personal influence. While many external variables cannot always be governed, we can absolutely maintain authority over our perspectives, responses, and reactions. The distinction and acceptance between what is controllable and what is not is the impetus of true personal power.

After establishing self-awareness and embracing the concept of accepting personal ownership, uncovering our underlying purpose is the next most crucial element in creating meaningful change. Consider the analogy that moving through life resembles driving a vehicle on a road trip. Think of every aspect of existence and each objective we yearn to achieve as specific locations on a map. It is the foundation of purpose that provides direction, serving as the guide for where to go and as the fuel that powers our actions toward reaching our preset destinations.

The same as traveling in uncharted territories without a map or global positioning system, living without a strong sense of direction means risking wandering aimlessly, taking wrong turns, getting lost, and wasting precious time and energy on dead-end routes. When an established sense of direction exists, our time and resources get used much more wisely and efficiently. With a clear indication of where we want to end up, burnout from backtracking, going in circles, hitting unnecessary detours, or finding arrival at undesirable locations becomes far more avoidable.

Unlike conventional maps that show one specific landscape, life maps represent numerous terrains such as health, relationships, career, and finances all at once. Your primary reason for being ensures that all paths connect and support each other rather than pulling in conflicting directions. Even when navigating with assistance, sometimes paths are closed or other obstacles appear. Things can even jump right out in front of you unexpectedly. This is where having purpose helps to slow you down, swerve, quickly recalculate, find alternative routes, or even determine if it is necessary to give up on reaching a location entirely.

Having a sense of direction is also what provides distance markers along our commutes, helping us recognize whether or not we are advancing and when we should be celebrating that we have reached specific checkpoints. This keeps motivation strong for the longer stretches ahead, and is all the more reason why we must understand that meaningful accomplishment is about enjoying the journey itself, not just about arriving at predetermined destinations. There is no guarantee that we will always make it to where we are going. That is why the real fun is in the adventures along the way.

To better aid us in meeting our end goals, though, sometimes examining other people's past voyages in detail proves worthwhile, as they may offer pertinent insights that can save us time and spare us from unnecessary trouble. Think about a time when you found yourself lost while traveling somewhere. For most who have encountered this situation, it is common for them to feel overwhelmed, frustrated, or confused. This is where learning from those who have traversed to the same destinations you are aspiring to reach can present valuable information, as they typically unveil viable shortcuts to take or warnings about potential hazards to avoid. Examining the experiences of others closely, paired with how they match up to your own drive and plans, often provides guidance that will keep you headed on the right track.

However, where following proven strategies can certainly serve as a highly effective formula, sometimes you might find yourself in a position where you are the first person to charter new territory for everyone else. The wisdom lies in researching what others may have done or would do relative to your efforts, while maintaining the courage to blaze new trails when necessary. Understanding the differences between calculated risks and terrible ideas is essential, and knowing all of the variables you have to work with helps to keep your choices far more safe.

As you set off along on your journey, always keep in mind how the three pillars of self-awareness, personal accountability, and purpose work together synchronistically to create profound, lasting change. When combined, they shape your mental patterns and outlooks, and guide your emotional states and behaviors. Ultimately, it is your choices and actions that determine opportunities, accomplishments, and accolades.

Being aware of these principles is one thing, yet implementing them consistently is where most people encounter the greatest resistance. The majority struggle with developing awareness where they need it most, adopting the mindsets they need to embrace taking personal accountability, or with doing the work it takes to establish a deep individualized sense of purpose and direction.

Fear is usually the silent culprit behind this phenomenon, and is often the controlling factor rendering more decisions and indecisions than most people recognize. It frequently creates restrictive outlooks that sabotage advancement. Commonly paired with negative experiences, current societal pressures, or the expectations from others, the power of fear easily contributes to constraining, limited thought processes. Specific fears of failure, rejection, inadequacy, and even the fear of success function as common barriers to growth, breeding the internal narratives that make people feel inadequate, unworthy, unintelligent, or undisciplined. These anxieties trigger hesitation, self-doubt, and inaction, leaving individuals feeling helpless, hopeless, or paralyzed in inactivity.

This is why we must learn to control our thoughts and develop the mental approach that will allow us to overcome any restricting beliefs that have become ingrained into our subconscious minds over time. The real solution begins with the first principle we already reviewed: self-awareness. Once any nonserving psychological constructs are recognized, their cycle is immediately broken. When we are ignorant, we do not know. When we become enlightened, however, it becomes much harder to hide from the truth. From knowing, it is a conscious choice to accept personal responsibility and to embrace change. The power, though, is transferred to us, as we then have optimization data that allows us to replace our limiting beliefs and actions with empowering new ones that support our overall growth and success.

The first part of this work begins with cultivating inner feelings of self-confidence, trust, and determination. Without these attributes, self-diminishment can occur far too easily. This is exactly how people fall into patterns of abusing unhealthy coping mechanisms or even into developing addictive behaviors. Whether numbing emotions through substances, distraction, procrastination, or seeking external approval and validation from others, any of these aspects of self-suppression prevent countless people from reaching their greatest potential.

A crucial first step in avoiding these cycles is understanding the fundamental connection between their thoughts, feelings, and the reality they create.

Consider the theory that thoughts generate feelings, which then act as signals to broadcast desires to the world.

The world does not discriminate based on what is perceived to be positive, negative, or indifferent. It responds to whatever consistently captures attention and emotional energy. Think of this process like the mind functioning as an internet browser. Your perpetual thinking represents website addresses being typed into the search bar, directing where mental focus lands. Each thought acts like typing in a specific web address that tells the universe exactly what kind of outcomes to deliver.

Just like a computer browser, you can have multiple tabs open at once, with different thoughts running simultaneously in the background. Sometimes wild or random thoughts get typed in, but these typically get deleted or replaced when they do not receive focused attention and emotional energy. The thoughts that remain open the longest and receive the most concentrated focus are the ones that eventually load into reality.

Your feelings, combined with subsequent actions or inactions, function as the "enter" key that transmits these requests. When you think about something repeatedly while feeling strongly about it, you are essentially hitting that "enter" button and requesting that specific type of experience to load into your screen. That screen represents your reality and what actually appears before your eyes in your daily life.

The key insight here is that this system responds to consistency and emotional intensity, not to whether you want or do not want something. Fear-based thoughts accompanied by strong emotions get the same response as hope-filled thoughts with strong emotions. The universe simply delivers more of whatever receives the most focused attention and feeling from the mind.

The problem most people face is constantly switching between different web addresses without allowing any single page sufficient time to load completely. They rapidly type in new thoughts, change course before anything can download and display, then enter in something else entirely. This cycle repeats endlessly, where nothing continues to fully load or actualize in reality. This mirrors how most approach their day-to-day aspirations by constantly shifting focus, jumping between ideas without maintaining concentration on a single vision long enough for it to materialize.

Whatever perpetually captures focus expands in our reality. Whether you view this through the lens of neuroscience, psychology, faith-based beliefs, or personal observation, this concept remains consistent across different worldviews. Research in neuroplasticity shows how repeated thoughts literally rewire brain pathways. Confirmation bias demonstrates how we notice evidence that supports our existing beliefs. The reticular activating system explains how our minds filter information to match what we are already thinking about.

Some may see this as divine providence responding to prayer and intention. Others view it as quantum physics or universal energy, while some explain it purely through cognitive psychology and behavioral science. The way we see it, the underlying explanation matters far less than the practical application. Regardless of your worldview or the mechanism you believe drives these results, one truth remains consistent: purpose-driven thinking, conviction, and aligned action create life-changing opportunities.

This science becomes the foundation as we begin personal transformation by focusing on optimizing both your internal and external approaches. This encompasses how you view yourself, the world around you, and the overall actions you choose to take.

Now that the fundamental power of mindset is clear, in the following chapter, we will start by learning how to organize the mind while gaining clarity through "The Mind Dump," a breakthrough exercise that will immediately shift how you think and operate. This powerful technique takes the mental clutter out of your head and puts it onto paper, taking any overwhelming flood of ideas, desires, goals, and responsibilities that may be circulating in your mind and making it into something completely manageable. This exercise is the catalyst for compartmentalizing thoughts and identifying the most significant priorities. Get ready to feel the relief and clarity that comes from finally organizing the mental world.

CHAPTER 2:
THE POWER OF
THE MIND DUMP

Most people either lack a clear idea of what they actually desire most in life or they struggle to organize their thoughts and beliefs in ways that lead to decisive, methodical action. This cognitive clutter influences indecision, creates overwhelming feelings, and becomes one of the primary culprits that keeps us stuck in place.

"The Mind Dump" is the first of three core transformational exercises introduced in this book. It has been designed to help gain direction, establish top priorities, and provide a plan to begin taking immediate, meaningful action. This represents the beginning portion of your direct hands-on experience and serves as the first step toward identifying and achieving your most significant wants, desires, and aspirations. Completing this exercise will create space for motivation and focused effort. Here, it is essential to be totally honest about what ideas may be occupying your mental space.

Critical to success in any area of life is proper initial planning. It is easy to overthink or feel as though ideas may be too big, or even too small. This exercise eliminates those concerns by removing all filters and limitations. While simple in nature, its impact can prove to be extremely profound.

The objective is to take every pressing idea from your mind and get it clearly laid out on paper. Writing down your ideas drastically increases the likelihood of achieving them by providing structure and accountability. By transferring your thoughts from your head into a visual representation, you can manage them much easier. Instead of chaos swirling in your mind, you can now see everything clearly and process it with greater emotional clarity. This allows you to move more effectively into the next steps of prioritizing your ideas to create an effective plan of action for the items that are most urgent and important to you.

The steps are straightforward. Write down what needs to be accomplished, what is hoped for, and what feels important, regardless of the size or scope. This could range from something small, like washing your car or doing laundry, to bigger life pursuits such as learning a new language, starting a business, or writing a book. Other examples might include getting a new car, hiring a maid, traveling to new destinations, finding a romantic partner, losing weight, creating a workout plan, making more money, starting a gratitude journal, volunteering more, or launching your own business. Where the possibilities are vast, the key is getting every aspiration out of your mind and onto paper without overthinking or censoring yourself.

Not all dreams, desires, or ideas need to be materialistic. They can include wanting better relationships, contributing to community causes, learning new skills, or creating meaningful experiences. What matters most is that your wishes reflect genuine authenticity. While writing them down, take a moment to reflect on why they hold significance for you. Also, be mindful that your wants should reflect your own personal values and aspirations. Be conscious about not chasing visions shaped by the need to please others, gain validation, or live up to societal expectations of success. The more honest and complete your "Mind Dump," the more powerfully this exercise can serve you.

When performing this exercise, we strongly recommend using a pen or pencil and writing by hand rather than typing thoughts electronically. Handwriting engages the brain in ways that improve memory, comprehension, and creative thinking. Writing by hand also slows the process just enough to help fully connect with what is being recorded. Research suggests using red-colored pens or pencils can help with paying more attention to detail and memorizing information, while blue colors can help stimulate more creative thinking. Playing classical or instrumental music at lower volumes while writing may also enhance your focus and creativity.

It is important to note that this exercise is not just a one-time activity. "The Mind Dump" can be used anytime feelings of overwhelm or uncertainty arise. Regularly clearing your mental space creates a better ability to refine priorities, eliminate distractions, and stay in alignment with your most important objectives. Over time, this can become a habit that helps you maintain focus and motivation, regardless of what challenges appear.

Once the "The Mind Dump" is complete, notice how you feel, and see if you notice any immediate sense of relief. Then review what was written to spot potential repeating patterns, priorities, and desires that may not have been as obvious before.

This newfound clarity is a great place to begin, but on its own, it is not always enough. To create real and lasting transformation, this raw list must be paired with a single, driving purpose. Purpose serves as the filter that helps you determine what matters most and what can wait. It reveals the aims that may best be pursued now to advance your biggest picture mission versus the endeavors that should be temporarily set aside.

We have found that once you have uncovered your purpose and realized an extreme level of focus and clarity, motivation, commitment, and discipline come more naturally as a byproduct. Disciplined action promotes consistency, and it is consistent effort that drives progress and meaningful results. Having a deep sense of purpose will drive your actions. When you know the true *why* behind any of your main intentions, the answers for what to do and how to do it will more clearly reveal themselves. Combining this understanding with the wisdom from this book will help you maximize your efforts.

However, it is important to recognize that not all of your aspirations will connect directly to your true inner purpose. Some may support it indirectly, while others may require attention for different reasons, such as deadlines, personal obligations, or matters of health and safety. Some may involve ensuring key areas of life, or the people within it, are not neglected. Others can include desires that may enhance your quality of life and contribute to overall well-being. The key is mastering balance between all of your initiatives while identifying the most pertinent priorities that will sustain overall growth, happiness, and purpose.

To further support you, this is precisely why developing a Chief Aim Statement becomes so essential. In the next chapter, insights from your "Mind Dump" will be used to craft a compelling Chief Aim that will serve as a guiding force, allowing you to better examine how to take decisive, methodical action toward the life that you dream of most. This purpose-driven approach is designed to bring greater direction to all of your hopes and aspirations.

The insights in this book provide everything needed to start making real progress right now. However, the full *Tilting The Balance™: A Guided Workbook for Clarity, Purpose, and Transformation* takes these concepts to a significantly deeper level with our "10 Categories of Life" framework that helps compartmentalize and structure desires into objectives in a way that makes prioritization and implementation far easier to manage. When you are ready to advance further and access our complete system, visit www.TiltingTheBalance.com/BuyNow to order a copy of our workbook.

For now, completing your "The Mind Dump" in this copy alone provides the foundation needed for you to move forward with a tremendous amount of newfound clarity. For your convenience, we have provided a dedicated template on the following pages for you to perform this exercise. If you do not have the physical copy of this book, or if printing the provided template from our website at www.TiltingTheBalance.com/Templates is not possible, a clean, blank sheet of paper will work just as well.

Now, before moving to the next chapter, take a moment to pause, find a quiet space free of distractions, turn on some classical or instrumental music, and allow yourself the sufficient time that it takes to effectively complete this exercise. You will know when the process is finished when it feels like everything has been emptied from your mind and onto the paper before you.

However, be mindful that new thoughts and ideas may very well continue to emerge, both during this exercise and as you continue reading through this book. When that happens, simply go back and add them to your list. This particular list is not ever intended to be set in stone. You can always add to it or adjust it at any time, and you likely always will be, as our lives, desires, and circumstances are ever changing.

Afterwards, you will be ready to continue to the next chapter to learn about how to structure and harness the power of utilizing a Chief Aim Statement. We hope you enjoy discovering what matters most to you, and we look forward to seeing you in the next chapter!

CHAPTER 3:
THE POWER OF DEFINING YOUR CHIEF AIM

Now that "The Mind Dump" has been completed, there should be a greater understanding about what you desire most in life. As we have covered, this insight alone is not enough. To create real transformation, the magic lies in refining your thoughts and focusing your energy toward a singular, driving purpose. This is where taking the time to create a Chief Aim Statement can drastically benefit you.

A Chief Aim is more than just a goal. It is a declaration of your deepest desires, backed by commitment, strategy, self-confidence, and belief. It serves as the guiding force that shapes how you make decisions, prioritize time, and take intentional action. It is also designed to help you build trust in your abilities to make your dreams a reality. Without a compelling sense of purpose, even the most ambitious people can struggle to overcome uncertainty, inconsistency, and distractions. This is where a Chief Aim Statement can directly aid in establishing a more concrete direction for your life.

The concept of a Chief Aim was made famous by Napoleon Hill in his 1937 classic, *Think and Grow Rich*. He outlined six fundamental steps that transform someone from feeling lost or misguided into a person with burning desire and the ability to achieve tangible results. While Napoleon Hill presented this concept primarily in terms of financial objectives, the principle itself applies to every area of life. Whether your goal is to improve your health, strengthen relationships, build a business, or rise as a leader, the same process of defining a decisive, specific target and reinforcing it daily serves to be just as effective.

Many accomplished individuals in recent history have credited *Think and Grow Rich* as a foundational influence in their achievements. Media mogul Oprah Winfrey has spoken about how the teachings shaped her mindset, while entrepreneur Daymond John, founder of FUBU and *Shark Tank* investor, attributes his rise from humble beginnings to these principles. Martial artist and actor Bruce Lee famously wrote his own version of this declaration, detailing his goal of earning ten million dollars by being the highest-paid Asian actor in the United States, years before it became his reality. Renowned personal development coach Tony Robbins has also acknowledged the impact Hill's work had on his journey.

Hill's approach focuses the mind with clarity, emotion, visualization, and repetition. These dynamics work together to align thought with desired outcomes. By vividly declaring and experiencing exactly what you want, by when, and what shall be done and given in return for it, ahead of its actual manifestation, intention is signaled to both your subconscious mind and the universe. This constant focus works to aid in attracting the people, resources, and opportunities that support your aspirations.

CREATING YOUR CHIEF AIM STATEMENT: A SIX-STEP PROCESS

To aid you in structuring your own statement, we are going to walk through Hill's six steps using a specific example to provide further clarity. Whether your vision involves building a company that globally changes lives, creates individual financial freedom, or simply allows the ability to make a comfortable living doing what brings fulfillment, these are part of the variables to decide in the initial phases of crafting your statement.

This is where you must start, identifying what your end goals are. This is how you harness your deepest inner wishes and transform them from abstract ideas into actionable plans, guidelines, and results.

Before diving deep into the six steps, it is essential to ensure your Chief Aim is built upon a foundation that aligns with who you are and what brings you the utmost fulfillment. The most successful people understand that achievement without authenticity often leads to emptiness. This is why the Japanese concept of Ikigai proves invaluable in this process.

Ikigai means "reason for being" and harmonizes four essential elements: what you love, what you excel at, what the world needs, and what you can be compensated for. When your Chief Aim incorporates these elements, it serves more than a goal; it becomes a calling. Without this alignment, even the most precisely crafted statement may not lead to meaningful achievements.

Consider someone who pursues financial goals based solely on earning potential without considering their passions or strengths. Even if they succeed, they risk attaining wealth that feels empty or unfulfilling. Conversely, focusing entirely on what energizes you without regard for market value or world impact may lead to struggles with financial stability or maintaining relevance in the marketplace.

As you prepare to craft your statement, reflect on these questions and your Ikigai answers: What activities make you feel most alive and energized? What natural strengths do you possess that others frequently acknowledge? How can you contribute value to others in ways that solve significant, real-world problems?

This exploration ensures your Chief Aim reflects not just what you want to achieve, but who you are at your core. It provides the foundation for the impact and legacy you wish to create through your endeavors. For a comprehensive Ikigai worksheet that guides you through discovering your authentic "reason for being," along with additional resources for crafting mission and vision statements, visit www.TiltingTheBalance.com/Statements. These resources work together to create a complete strategic framework that aligns your Chief Aim with your deeper purpose and long-term vision.

With these fundamentals established, let us now walk through the six steps for creating your statement. For our sample, we will use the example that the dream is to become a highly successful real estate investor.

Step 1: Fix in Your Mind the Exact Amount of Money You Desire

Your declaration must begin with your name followed by a precise monetary goal. Vague desires like "I want to be rich" or "I shall have lots of money" are not precise enough for success. You must set an exact financial amount that your mind can focus on.

Example: "I, [Your Name], will have in my possession $1,000,000."

This specificity creates a measurable idea for your subconscious mind and is critical in shaping your decisions and actions. If you are wondering how high to set your goal initially, Napoleon Hill established clear principles for this benchmark. Your goal must be specific, and you must believe in it enough that your subconscious accepts it as possible. If the number feels too small, it likely cannot ignite a deep, burning internal desire. If it feels impossibly large, it is more likely to be dismissed as fantastical. The sweet spot is an idea that excites you, pushes you outside your comfort zone, and still feels achievable with focused effort and faith. The beauty is, once you do reach a proposed target, you can always create an updated statement and build again from there.

Step 3: Establish a Definite Date

Goals without clear deadlines lack urgency. Therefore, just as you set a precise financial amount, you must set an exact date for achieving the outcome as defined in your statement.

Example: "I will achieve this by December 31, 20XX."

This deadline creates accountability and gives the mind a fixed target. A concrete timeline enhances your ability to make strategic decisions and maintain discipline in daily actions.

Step 4: Create a Definite Plan and Begin Immediately

A dream without a plan is most often just a wish. To bring dreams to life, we must design and implement methodical approaches and take consistent action, even when the best paths forward feel uncertain. For this step, you are going to complete a general outline for how you shall achieve your goal. It does not need to be a detailed strategy at this stage. For our real estate investment business example, here are some potential plan options:

- Continually educate myself on market trends and investment strategies
- Secure numerous, highly beneficial funding options for investment property financing
- Build a powerhouse team of expert real estate agents, property inspectors, contractors, wholesalers, property managers, and industry professionals who all operate with the utmost integrity

- Become masterful at analyzing profitable investment opportunities
- Develop robust systems to ensure all aspects of my operations run smoothly for everyone involved

Overthinking typically leads to procrastination. The key is to get started, because even small actions can build momentum and compound over time, revealing new options, opportunities, and outcomes. The most accomplished people usually begin before they feel completely ready and stay flexible enough to adjust along the way. True mastery lies in finding the balance between overplanning and underplanning, and developing the wisdom to know when to advance, pause, refine or abandon certain initiatives.

CHIEF AIM STATEMENT WORKSHEET

With all of these insights, you are now ready to begin crafting your very own statement. We have created a detailed worksheet that aids you in the process:

Take time now to work through each step, developing a personal statement:

Step 1: My Exact Financial Goal
I, (Your Name), will have in my possession $_____

Step 2: What I Will Give in Return
In return, I will _____

Step 3: My Deadline
I will achieve this by _____(Insert Exact Date)_____

Step 4: My Plan (List the most impactful, specific actions possible)
1. _____
2. _____
3. _____
4. _____
5. _____

Step 5: Write Out a Clear, Concise Statement
Now, combine all previous steps into a written declaration that reinforces the vision. This step transforms the individual components into one powerful, comprehensive statement that captures the complete intention. When crafting your statement, remember that your Chief Aim should be clear, memorable, and inspiring. It should be easy to read aloud with conviction, capture the essence without overwhelming detail, and flow naturally when spoken. You may choose to include every detail from your planning, or streamline your statement to be more compelling and memorable by focusing on the most impactful commitments and actions.

Example Statement: "I, [Your Name], will have in my possession $1,000,000 by December 31, 20XX. In return, I will dedicate the majority of my time to analyzing and acquiring profitable properties, building exceptional relationships with real estate professionals, and always creating value for my tenants and business partners. I will continuously educate myself, secure beneficial financing, build a powerhouse team, master property analysis, and develop systems that ensure success for everyone involved. I will consistently take action toward my plan and will always embrace every opportunity for growth."

The key is finding the balance between comprehensive coverage of your commitments and creating a statement that ignites burning desire each time you read it.

Keep in mind that this is just one example. Your declaration can take many forms depending on what matters most to you. For some, it could be winning an award, becoming a world champion in a sport, or inventing a product that revolutionizes the world. You may dream of writing a best-selling book, building a thriving enterprise, traveling to meaningful destinations, helping animals or the environment, or achieving personal goals such as mastering a skill or completing a meaningful accomplishment. Whatever your answers, your statement should align with the outcomes that matter most to you personally.

Step 6: Read Your Statement Aloud Twice Daily

Once your statement feels complete, the real science is in utilizing repetition to ingrain your objectives into the subconscious, aligning your thoughts and actions with the belief in the achievement of your desires. To develop this deep sense of belief, Napoleon Hill recommends reading your statement aloud with conviction each morning upon waking and each evening before retiring to best reinforce your belief and alignment with your goals.

For maximum impact, it is suggested you pair your approach with Hill's Self-Confidence Formula, a pre-written declaration that affirms your abilities, reinforces persistence, and conditions your mind to act with determination. Napoleon Hill advises reciting it aloud at least once daily. You may choose to read the Self-Confidence Formula before your statement, which primes your mind with belief and conviction. Or you may prefer to do so afterwards, reinforcing your goals with a declaration of confidence and self-trust. Experiment with various approaches and timing to discover which strategy resonates most with you. While we suggest the mornings to help set the tone for your day, you may also recite it at any point during your waking hours to strengthen your alignment and belief, as consistency is more important than timing. Hill's Self-Confidence Formula is included at the end of this chapter for your reference.

The last critical component of this process is to ensure that, in the evenings, after reciting your Chief Aim Statement aloud (along with the Self-Confidence Formula if you choose), you spend time vividly visualizing your dreams as if they are already accomplished. Napoleon Hill taught that this approach of seeing and feeling yourself already in possession of your desire is essential. We recommend setting aside up to thirty minutes daily to participate in this exercise, although Hill did not specify an exact duration.

To properly execute the practice of visualization, you must begin by creating a detailed image of what achievement looks and feels like for you. Clearly see it in your mind and step into the moment as though it has already happened. This could be something like seeing yourself logging into your bank account and seeing the exact amount of your goal deposited. Or perhaps you visualize yourself walking through the front door of the home you have always dreamed of owning, feeling the keys in your hand as you turn to see your loved one's faces light up with joy. Maybe you see yourself standing on stage receiving an award for your achievements, hearing the applause and feeling the weight of a trophy in your hands. You might envision opening an acceptance letter to your dream university, or shaking hands with a business partner as you sign a contract that changes everything for your company. The possibilities are endless, but the key is to create a vivid picture that captures your deepest emotions and makes the achievement feel absolutely real.

This very method has been used successfully by many accomplished individuals. One of the best examples is the famous actor Jim Carrey who successfully applied this very approach. He wrote himself a check for ten million dollars years before his breakthrough and carried it in his wallet while visualizing himself receiving that exact amount for his acting services. When his career reached new heights with his role in the 1994 award-winning movie *Dumb and Dumber*, he earned precisely that sum. Perhaps you'll decide to hold a check written for the amount you set, just as Carrey did?

To further enhance and optimize your practice, your visualization routines can become much more expansive when you can go deep into every detail. When you finally actualize the moment where you have achieved your desires, what are you wearing at that time? What colors surround you? Who is with you, and what are they saying? Where are you? Are you inside somewhere or outdoors? What does the scenery look like around you? What sounds do you hear? Is there applause, music, or a voice announcing your name? What do you feel physically, such as temperature, textures, or perhaps the weight of an object in your hand? Are there any tastes or smells present? What specific emotions are you experiencing in this exact moment?

As you build the imagery of your dream come true, be sure to engage all of your senses. The more vivid and specific this scene is, the more your subconscious mind can accept it and the better it can begin working to convert your visions into your reality.

These collective steps have a genuine ability to condition your mind for achievement. By repeatedly affirming your statement, the Self-Confidence Formula, and visualizing your results with conviction, a transformation in behaviors, identity, and outcomes can occur. Most people fail to live out their deepest desires because they do not follow through on the work it takes to reinforce the belief that their dreams are even possible to achieve. By consistently utilizing this practice, it helps you overcome self-doubt, build confidence, and remain aligned with your purpose and actions.

By following these steps, you establish a structured, personalized, daily reminder of what is being worked toward. This collectively aids you in maintaining focus, motivation, and discipline.

With your statement developed, the natural progression is to begin implementing it into your daily routine. To optimize your results, this approach must become a habit. Massive goals can feel overwhelming, which is why planning your early objectives and measuring your progress is essential. This is where our "*The 3-4-30 Challenge*SM" comes into effect. It is our revolutionary framework designed to transform ideas into actionable goals while keeping you focused within shorter-term intervals. By breaking aspirations into smaller, measurable, and more manageable steps and pairing them with structured accountability partnerships, you create the conditions for meaningful and rapid growth. Both your Chief Aim Statement and "*The 3-4-30 Challenge*SM" are powerful tools, but their value depends entirely on you. They will only transform your life if you take responsibility for utilizing them consistently.

Before moving into the next chapter, take the time to begin drafting your Chief Aim Statement. If you feel you would benefit from hands-on support, we are here to guide you through the process of optimizing it and implementing it into your life. Visit www.TiltingTheBalance.com/LiveLearning to explore our coaching services and learn how we can support your journey to help you accomplish what matters most.

Below is an extract from Napoleon Hill's *Think and Grow Rich* (re-published in 2007):

Self-Confidence Formula

I know that I have the ability to achieve the object of my Definite Purpose in life, therefore, I DEMAND of myself persistent, continuous action toward its attainment, and I here and now promise to render such action.

I realize the dominating thoughts of my mind will eventually reproduce themselves in outward, physical action, and gradually transform themselves into physical reality, therefore, I will concentrate my thoughts for thirty minutes daily, upon the task of thinking of the person I intend to become, thereby creating in my mind a clear mental picture of that person.

I know through the principle of auto-suggestion, any desire that I persistently hold in my mind will eventually seek expression through some practical means of attaining the object back of it, therefore, I will devote ten minutes daily to demanding of myself the development of SELF-CONFIDENCE.

I have clearly written down a description of my DEFINITE CHIEF AIM in life, and I will never stop trying, until I shall have developed sufficient self-confidence for its attainment.

I fully realize that no wealth or position can long endure, unless built upon truth and justice, therefore, I will engage in no transaction which does not benefit all whom it affects. I will succeed by attracting to myself the forces I wish to use, and the cooperation of other people. I will induce others to serve me, because of my willingness to serve others. I will eliminate hatred, envy, jealousy, selfishness, and cynicism, by developing love for all humanity, because I know that a negative attitude toward others can never bring me success. I will cause others to believe in me, because I will believe in them, and in myself.

I will sign my name to this formula, commit it to memory, and repeat it aloud once a day, with full FAITH that it will gradually influence my THOUGHTS and ACTIONS so that I will become a self-reliant, and successful person.

(Signed Your Full Name & Date Completed)

CHAPTER 4:
THE POWER OF THIRTY-DAY CHALLENGES

Now that you have completed your "Mind Dump" and crafted your Chief Aim Statement, you should have a much clearer conception of what you want most. You have defined your purpose and set a clear direction, but this formula alone does not create results. Action does.

The biggest obstacle between you and your objectives is not a lack of desire, it is the failure to take consistent, structured action. This is precisely why we created "*The 3-4-30 Challenge*^{SM}." This framework bridges the gap between knowing what you want and actually making it happen.

Most people overestimate what they can accomplish in a day but underestimate what becomes possible in thirty days with a clear plan, accountability, and persistent effort. This presents an opportunity to take everything you have uncovered about your vision, priorities, and purpose in order to channel it into measurable progress.

The reality is that most of us struggle with maintaining consistency. We set goals with the best intentions, but without proper structure and ways to measure progress, our efforts often fade into the background of our everyday lives. This common cycle contributes to anxiety, frustration, limiting beliefs, and causes the majority of people to give up pursuing their desires. Because major aspirations can feel so extensive, impractical, or sometimes even improbable, that diminishing sense of our desired outcomes being so far out of reach typically hinders or halts us from ever moving toward them. "*The 3-4-30 Challenge*^{SM}" presents a viable solution, converting aspirations into action by breaking down overwhelming goals into small, measurable, and achievable short-term milestones while promoting ongoing accountability every step of the way.

At its core, "*The 3-4-30 Challenge*^{SM}" follows a simple formula. You must choose up to three priority goals, commit to executing them for thirty days, and check in with an accountability partner at least four times per month (or up to four times per week or even more if you choose for added support). Up to three primary goals, at least one meeting per week, for a period of thirty days; 3-4-30. This balance of structure and flexibility has the ability to reinvent your progress without the steps feeling overly rigid or overwhelming.

To understand how this method works, think of making a decision to climb a mountain. Picture yourself standing at the bottom, looking up, only to see a layer of clouds blocking the rest of the view. For many people, this is exactly what happens when they think about their most significant ideas. The end vision of where they want to land versus where they are beginning feels unclear, and the gap seems overbearing or even impossible. That perception is what paralyzes most from ever getting started. "*The 3-4-30 Challenge*^{SM}" breaks down the process, removes the fog, and puts everything into a visible line of sight, making the improbable feel manageable and possible.

Thirty days provides an ideal timeframe for this to occur. It is short enough to see an end point to inspire effort and maintain motivation, and yet is just long enough to make progress, experience immediate results, and to even begin reforming unfavorable habits and limiting beliefs. When paired with the power of ongoing accountability, this digestible approach increases follow-through substantially.

The idea behind "*The 3-4-30 Challenge*^{SM}" is actually what sparked the development of *Tilting The Balance*™. We designed our entire system around what encourages others and promotes progress, and found that structured thirty-day challenges can help create real change faster than any other implementation strategies we have personally experimented with.

Every successful challenge begins with concrete direction, most effectively organized through the "S.M.A.R.T. Goals" framework. This ensures that each goal is Specific (clearly defined), Measurable (trackable with concrete metrics), Achievable (realistic given your current situation), Relevant (aligned with your priorities), and Time-bound (with definite deadlines within the thirty-day period).

For example, say you consume sugary sodas daily, and it has been a longstanding goal to eliminate them from your diet entirely. However, after numerous unsuccessful attempts to quit, the feat now seems impossible. This is common for anyone who has pursued a goal and fallen short, especially if they have had numerous tries. If it seems too unrealistic to push yourself to the limits by immediately setting the goal to stop drinking them altogether, you could set your first thirty-day challenge to scale back your intake to only be allowed to drink them on certain days of the week, or you could limit yourself to only drinking a specific amount each week. These approaches inspire growth. As you gradually build awareness, self-confidence, and experience results, it can inspire you to make further incremental increases over time.

This balanced formula works for just about any initiative. As another example, let us say your goal is to master incorporating the Chief Aim practice into your daily routine by reciting it paired with the Self-Confidence Formula each morning, followed by the Chief Aim again in the evenings along with a set time for visualizing success. You could start small by dedicating one day in the first week, then add a second day in week two, a third in week three, and a fourth in week four. Over time, you can expand to daily practice with longer visualization sessions, eventually making it a lasting part of your lifestyle. This is the same step-up process that applies whether you are pursuing short-term benchmarks or building long-term transformation.

To effectively utilize this strategy, we advise recurrently embarking upon new challenges every thirty days. By doing this, the beauty of the "*The 3-4-30 Challenge*^{SM}" provides the flexibility to structure "S.M.A.R.T. Goals" in a manner that is manageable based on where you currently are at any given time. As your circumstances and feelings change, you can set objectives to go all in, go all out, wean yourself off of things, or gradually introduce new actions or activities into your life.

Short-term aims might involve completing a personal project such as finishing a painting, reorganizing your living space, submitting a work report, or completing a school assignment. Some of these require speed and focus within your thirty day periods. While some shorter-term initiatives may not ever become necessary after completion or perhaps may not reappear for quite a length of time after, others may continually call for your direct attention once or up to several times per week, and some can require ongoing, daily repetition.

More long-term priorities, such as improving financial stability, strengthening relationships, or achieving career advancement, often benefit most from setting steady milestones. These could include meal prepping on designated days, deep cleaning on predetermined weekends, scheduling regular reviews of various tasks and expenses, committing to physical activity a set number of days each week, or avoiding certain foods at planned intervals. These goals may seem simple, but their compounding effect is massive when paired with consistent action and accountability.

That is how you climb the mountain one step at a time. It is just like drops of water falling from a faucet and collecting into a bucket. Each step upward may not feel impactful on its own. Every single little droplet may seem insignificant. As time unfolds, though, eventually, the mountain will be scaled, and the bucket will be filled. Depending on the endeavor, it can boil down to how much intensity you choose to operate with. Maybe you decide to climb faster, or increase the pressure on the faucet. Whichever the case, you have to move, or turn that faucet on. It becomes about consistency, persistence, and your commitment to keep moving forward.

Human nature and our desires for instant gratification can tend to influence us to want to take our progress immediately from ground zero to the highest levels of how we envision our best selves. In most instances, it is like working out at the gym, but mentally. It takes time to gain momentum and to develop the muscle of confidence and belief that our most intimidating dreams are possible to achieve. Keep in mind, some of our habits become aspects of our identities. We are not merely always overcoming our decisions and behaviors when we are focused on bigger picture initiatives, we could also be working to form entirely new self-images.

Think of it like being in a game of tug-of-war with yourself. The old version of you is going to try to pull you back to hold you in place while the new vision of your desired self pulls against it. The question is, how do you gain the edge so that the person you want to become most wins?

This is how the psychology behind *"The 3-4-30 Challenge*SM*"* is so simple and powerful. If you can consolidate discouraging ideas into more minimal, achievable targets, as automaticity takes hold (the process where behaviors become automatic through repetition), resistance is removed, and you can amplify your efforts. This becomes your anchor, the strongest position on your new team in the game of tug-of-war against your prior self. It also supports you when you turn up that faucet pressure (meaning increasing the intensity of your efforts) by ensuring there are no leaks in the pipe. When your actions are not diminished, you can work and flow more freely, better preserving your precious time, energy, resources, and self-confidence.

To better conserve yourself and ensure progress, it is also vital to recognize that there is a real threshold to how much change can be effectively managed at one time. Lasting transformation comes from remaining focused on a few meaningful adjustments rather than attempting to tackle everything at once. For this reason, we advise concentrating on the single most impactful aims as you go.

That is why the "3" in our "*3-4-30 Challenge*^{SM}" suggests that you limit yourself to no more than three critical initiatives. If any of them happen to be habit-focused, we have actually found it is best to work on no more than one or two at a time.

Now that we have covered how to structure goals effectively, the next critical dynamic is applying the element of ongoing ownership. This is why "*The 3-4-30 Challenge*^{SM}" integrates accountability partnerships into your approach. This system helps to keep you aware, motivated, disciplined, and drastically optimizes your chances of success.

Selecting the right accountability partnerships is the next crucial component for achieving results. The most ideal partners must be supportive, reliable, and honest. They should care about your progress, remain committed to checking in regularly, help you stay focused, hold you highly responsible, and genuinely question your decisions when necessary.

If you happen to fall short of a goal, your partner can serve you best by encouraging candid communication that promotes critical thought and deep reflection on how and why it happened. They must have both the ability and your blessing to do this effectively, as each is necessary to help you reach the highest levels of awareness.

There is certainly an intrinsic balance where your accountability partner must hold you responsible without allowing easy outs or excuses, while also not being so harsh that it becomes counterproductive. Setting boundaries upfront with your accountability partners is exceptionally suggested. We recommend you lay out whether you want them to be softer and sugarcoat feedback, take a drill sergeant approach, or strike a balance between the two approaches based on what best motivates you.

Your accountability partners do not need to be simultaneously participating in their own individual "*3-4-30 Challenge*^{SM}." The most important factor is that they are genuine in their willingness to support you and meet with you regularly throughout yours. However, it is more ideal for any accountability partner to be doing their own "*3-4-30 Challenge*^{SM}" along with you, as this gives an equal chance for all to grow and build deeper camaraderie together. It also further promotes our philosophy that everyone should always be endeavoring upon their own "*3-4-30 Challenge*^{SM}" at all times.

As far as having multiple active partnerships, where you could certainly have different partners for various types of goals, create a greater support network, or have backup options if someone may be unavailable, we do not advise that approach. The reason is counterintuitive because it can actually complicate the initiative for everyone involved. What we have personally found best is to have either an intimate one-on-one partnership or be in groups of no more than five people. The larger meetings can have sessions that span several hours, and people can sometimes become rushed, interrupted, and their flows can become challenging to manage. More centralized groups tend to be more efficient (though they can certainly last for an hour or longer) and most importantly, they can open a space for greater depth of communication.

It is best practice to preschedule as many times and dates in advance as possible for each of your meetings. This allows you to remain more proactive versus reactive throughout your challenges. The key is to eliminate resistance by establishing when you will meet for your sessions before they occur. Leaving this unplanned is an easy recipe for them to be missed and to not follow through on your thirty-day goals.

When deciding who to partner with, you can choose close family members, friends, professional colleagues, or anybody else who has a growth mindset and who is enthusiastic to participate with you. However, if you work with people with whom you have strong personal relationships, this is an area where we recommend you exercise caution. Just as much as having them as your partners has the chance to bring you closer, sometimes when people are placed into environments of challenge for personal growth, it can create real tension. Also, just because you have an established connection with someone you feel could be ideal to work with, it does not mean they may automatically want to be your partner in return. You must remember that only you are responsible for your own growth and development, and that other people are entitled to control their own, along with their reasons for why they may or may not want to join you.

Whomever you select, they need to be somebody you are comfortable being vulnerable with and who will respect keeping your aspirations and the honest thoughts you share private. Sadly, some people can use your thoughts or shortcomings to weaponize them against you based on their own insecurities. These are all real factors to consider when opting to have somebody participate with you.

Regardless, you never know the types of relationships these periods may help you build. They can strengthen bonds with people you already share close connections with, and they can also lead to meaningful new relationships with individuals you may not have known as well before. Even in the worst case scenario, for those who may not end up respecting your efforts or privacy along the way, you will gain the benefit of discovering who genuinely supports you. What matters most is that you do your best and remain true to yourself. As long as your actions operate from a place of integrity, this process gives you the confidence to stand firmly in your own truth, free from the weight of other people's thoughts or opinions.

If you do not have an accountability partner or someone you feel would be a strong fit to support you, we also have this basis covered for you. We host accountability communities where you can meet like-minded individuals who are on their own personal missions to participate in their own "*3-4-30 Challenge*[SM]." You can get connected today at www.TiltingTheBalance.com/AccountabilityPartners.

Once you have selected your partnerships, effective sessions for "*The 3-4-30 Challenge*[SM]" involve three primary components. The first meeting should outline each "S.M.A.R.T. Goal" that every participant plans to accomplish. The subsequent meetings should review progress since the last check-in, address any obstacles or challenges that have arisen, and establish intentions along with the scheduled time and date for the next session. From there, it is the exciting time to commit fully to your priorities for the thirty-day duration. Remember that if an objective cannot realistically be completed in that timeframe, such as losing fifty pounds or attaining a degree or certification, it must be broken into smaller, measurable milestones that span consecutive challenges. This could mean aiming for one to two pounds of healthy weight loss per week, or selecting specific days each week to follow an exercise regimen or dietary protocol, with the understanding that consistent, proven activities will naturally produce desired results over time.

After your challenge concludes, you can choose to repeat or modify existing goals or to establish new ones for the next one to follow. The focus is always about progress, not perfection. Therefore, another one of the single most important aspects of this system is tracking your progress. This keeps your priorities visible every day and allows you to review pertinent data during your weekly accountability check-ins. Even if you do not fully achieve your targets, tracking your collective actions empowers you to better reflect on what worked, what did not, and what can or may need to be adjusted to further refine your strategy.

To practically keep track, we advise using a spreadsheet, a text message or email thread, or at minimum, a written log of each individual's initial preset "S.M.A.R.T. Goals," though we recommend utilizing technology or a method where everyone can easily access them in real time. Tracking weekly progress to see whether each participant's plans were met or not is an essential part of the process. This practice creates greater awareness and provides material for future reflection, much like a journal that documents growth over time.

Defining individual success should not be overly complicated, and is not only about the simple question of whether one accomplished their objectives. The definite measures built into your "S.M.A.R.T. Goals" will determine whether the process was truly successful. Even if there might have been some areas where actions fell short, if any quantifiable progress was made, then any increment of growth is better than none at all. Even a fraction of one percent worth of forward movement represents momentum that can still compound over time. One good decision can lead to another. However, this mindset and level of monitoring represents just another part of the equation.

The true essence of "*The 3-4-30 Challenge*SM" is centered around daily conscious living. It is not about being self-critical if you do not reach a target, or about inflating your ego when you do have personal victories. The power is in gaining the awareness and confidence of how to be at your best while striving to be your best self, and being there for others who may be working with you to do the same.

The real magic behind "*The 3-4-30 Challenge*SM" can happen when it becomes part of your active routine lifestyle. We urge you to build the habit of embarking upon a new "*3-4-30 Challenge*SM" every thirty days, continuing to always refine your strategy while remaining connected with accountability partners, groups, coaches, and any other supportive figures you can throughout your journey. The most productive people in the world tend to operate in structured cycles, turning steady effort into lasting habits that expand into extraordinary results. However you decide is best for you, whether starting small and gaining momentum or going the opposite direction and putting extreme challenges on yourself for thirty-day intervals, as soon as one thirty-day challenge ends, we advise you to immediately roll right into the next one.

Our mission here is to provide you with the best simplified insights possible to help you achieve real, lasting results without all the jargon, gimmicks, or overcomplication. We are giving you all the basics you need to get started with

"*The 3-4-30 Challenge*^{SM}" right away because we know how instantaneously and powerfully this method can begin to change and impact your life.

In closing, "*The 3-4-30 Challenge*^{SM}" is designed to prompt action, and is for doing, not just planning. You now have everything you need to set your intentions, find your accountability partners, and get started now, even with the simplest of goals. Do not wait around for "the perfect time." There is always an opportunity to refine and master your approach along the way, but you have to start first.

While you are certainly equipped with everything you need to gain transformative results now, for greater strategic insights on how to structure and organize your "*3-4-30 Challenge*^{SM}" in ways that make achievement significantly more automatic and effortless, we recommend gaining an understanding of how they intertwine with "The 10 Categories of Life" paired with all of the additional information contained within *Tilting The Balance*™: *A Guided Workbook for Clarity, Purpose, and Transformation*. You can always attain a copy of our workbook at www.TiltingTheBalance.com/BuyNow.

If you prefer expert guidance and want a more personalized experience with implementing your "*3-4-30 Challenge*^{SM}," our direct coaching services are available to help you. We offer both one-on-one and group coaching, and would be honored to serve as your accountability partner. We can aid you in properly structuring your "S.M.A.R.T. Goals" based on your personal circumstances and are prepared to help you maintain consistency every step of the way. You can learn more about how to get started today at www.TiltingTheBalance.com/LiveLearning.

Where "*The 3-4-30 Challenge*^{SM}" promotes structure, ongoing accountability, and continual progress, other key ingredients can also directly contribute to your long-term achievements. We will explore these in detail next as you continue to the next section on powerful mindset reinforcement practices.

CHAPTER 5:
REINFORCING YOUR MINDSET: PROVEN PRACTICES

There is a significant reason we started this journey together by focusing on the power of mindset. Achievement begins in the mind. Every action taken, every goal pursued, and every result obtained is first shaped by our thoughts. When our mental frameworks are misaligned with our approaches, our end results are far more likely to become diminished or inconsistent. Conversely, with a strong, empowering foundation of thought, the likelihood of reaching our desired outcomes becomes much more viable.

The challenge the majority of us face when working toward what we want most is not a lack of ambition or effort. The real issue is that we have not learned how to condition our minds for success. Without reinforcing the right thoughts, emotions, and beliefs, even the best strategies can prove ineffective.

Four of the most powerful practices for mental reconditioning are affirmations, visualization, meditation, and gratitude. These practices retrain the subconscious mind, helping individuals think, feel, and respond in ways that align with their values and desired results. While many dismiss them as superficial concepts, scientific research has consistently proven their effectiveness.

Affirmations can rewire limiting subconscious beliefs by replacing self-doubt with empowering thoughts, shifting the ways we make decisions and take action. Visualization can activate the same neural pathways as real-life experiences, programming the mind to expect achievement while reinforcing confidence. Meditation strengthens clarity and emotional control, reduces stress, enhances focus, and can make it easier to remain calm while taking decisive steps toward what we want most. The power of gratitude trains the brain to concentrate on abundance rather than lack, naturally guiding thoughts toward recognizing opportunities instead of dwelling on obstacles while simultaneously creating a deeper sense of appreciation for all positive aspects of life.

Mastering these practices does not replace effort, but makes the process of reaching outcomes far more fluid and sustainable. The mind begins to respond to the messages it repeatedly receives. This supports how developing the habit of utilizing affirmations, visualization, meditation, and gratitude can condition the mind for success. By aligning thoughts with goals, the right steps and opportunities are more likely to follow. When integrating these methods strategically into daily life, individuals are not just improving the ways they think; they are creating a mental environment where attaining anticipated results becomes increasingly probable.

Many people struggle to change their habits because they try to change their actions before working to change their thoughts about the actions they take. While these methods will not always replace the real hard work that can be involved, they can certainly help maintain forward momentum, making efforts easier by removing obstacles that exist only in perception. Often, what we label as difficulties are not true challenges at all, but are rather mere barriers we have created in our own minds. Genuine issues will always require our attention and resolution, but many times, by simply shifting our perspectives, many can be revealed as less daunting than they initially appeared.

For those of you who may be thinking all of this seems too abstract, skepticism of these fundamentals is common. Affirmations can be dismissed as ineffective because they feel forced or unnatural initially. However, the mind operates on repetition and consistency. Just as negative self-talk can turn automatic over time, positive affirmations can reshape internal dialogue through the same neurological pathways. The key difference lies in directing this inherent mental process toward empowering rather than limiting beliefs.

Visualizations can be seen as daydreaming, and meditation as a time-consuming endeavor where you also sit with your eyes shut with no tangible results. Even gratitude can be misunderstood and underestimated, viewed as contrived positivity rather than a genuine mindset shift. However, the science paired with the direct results behind these methods is undeniable. Extensive research has shown that rewiring subconscious beliefs leads to measurable improvements in performance, resilience, and emotional well-being. These practices serve as catalysts for deep mental transformation. Top athletes, executives, and entrepreneurs worldwide attribute their success to these approaches as essential components of their achievement. As the authors, we can personally attest that these practices have absolutely transformed our lives.

While the foundation of these methods is now clear, their journey of implementation for you can begin immediately. You can find guided meditations, visualization exercises, and affirmation practices on YouTube and through various online platforms. For gratitude, we suggest starting with a simple daily practice of writing down five specific things you appreciate, each morning right as you wake up and each evening just before bed. Many people also benefit from gratitude journals, apps, or even voice recordings of their daily reflections. These free resources provide an excellent starting point for experiencing the power of these practices firsthand.

If you are seeking further structured guidance and accelerated results, *Tilting The Balance*™: *A Guided Workbook for Clarity, Purpose, and Transformation* provides comprehensive frameworks for crafting personalized affirmations, designing effective visualization sequences, establishing sustainable meditation routines, and developing advanced gratitude techniques that create measurable, life-changing results. To purchase a copy of our workbook and gain access to these detailed implementation strategies to fast-track your mental reconditioning today, visit www.TiltingTheBalance.com/BuyNow. Thirty days provides an ideal timeframe for this to occur. It is short enough to see an end point to inspire effort and maintain motivation, and yet is just long enough.

CHAPTER 6:
STRUCTURING SUCCESS: ADDITIONAL IMPLEMENTATION PRACTICES THAT WORK

Developing the right mindset creates the foundation for success, but without structured execution, even the most empowering thoughts may not create meaningful or lasting results.

Many people struggle to follow through on their aspirations because they lack a system to hold themselves accountable. They usually rely solely on motivation, which tends to fluctuate daily, and set vague intentions that lack clear execution plans. When combined with the virtually inevitable distractions presented by daily life, this diminishes the consistent action and outcomes that people want most.

This reality is precisely why the most accomplished individuals do not rely solely on willpower. Instead, they create systems that reinforce consistency, progress, and achievement. They surround themselves with positive influences and work with coaches, mentors, and teammates who help them organize their time, establish strong habits, and protect their focus with firm boundaries.

In this chapter, we will explore four additional structural practices that complement and enhance everything you have already learned, providing even more detailed strategies to ensure follow-through on your aspirations. These elements work together to create the optimal system for lasting transformation.

First, we will examine hard scheduling, also known as time blocking, which is a proven strategy that organizes your calendar so the most important priorities remain a constant focus. Next, we will cover the power of routines, which automate progress by turning high-value actions into effortless habits. We will then discuss how imperative it is to set firm boundaries to protect your time, energy, and focus from both negativity and distractions. Lastly, we will explore the significance of your social influences, reviewing how the individuals and messages you expose yourself to most can either promote or hinder your growth.

Hard scheduling involves treating your most important activities like unmovable appointments. Rather than hoping to somehow find moments for what matters, you deliberately block out dedicated periods on your calendar for specific priorities. The beauty of this approach is that it works brilliantly across every area of life. You could reserve two hours each morning for exercise (6:00 - 8:00 A.M. as an example) to ensure your physical health never gets pushed aside by daily demands. Mental wellness practices like affirmations, meditations, gratitude, and visualization exercises, even your Chief Aim practice, can all become non-negotiable when given protected calendar slots.

This method proves equally effective for practical matters. Setting aside dedicated periods on Sunday afternoons for meal preparation eliminates weekday decision fatigue around food choices. Reserving Friday evenings for meaningful dates ensures your romantic relationships receive consistent attention despite busy calendars. Planning monthly financial reviews where you check account balances and pay or audit automated bills prevents money management from becoming reactive or stressful. Even recurring administrative tasks benefit from this approach. You can allocate time outdoors immersed in nature or participating in your favorite hobbies for mental clarity, designate periods to manage household chores and personal errands, or organize the next day's micro-tasks during the work week to dramatically improve your overall efficiency and peace of mind.

While hard scheduling regiments your calendar, routines eliminate the mental energy required for continuous decision-making. When beneficial actions become automatic, you no longer need to rely on as much brain power, motivation, or even the highest levels of discipline to maintain them. Your first routines immediately upon waking set the tone for your entire day. Rather than starting reactively by immediately checking text messages, emails, social media, or watching news, the best approach is to establish proactive morning practices that organize, energize, and emotionally center you. The same principle applies for the evening routines you implement when finalizing your day, as they help you wind down effectively and optimize preparations for tomorrow. You can create powerful routines at any point throughout your day to develop habits that make performing high-value behaviors nearly effortless. Many actions that initially require focused energy can eventually become as automatic as brushing your teeth, freeing mental capacity for more advanced challenges and complex decisions.

Implementing new routines to form habits requires intention, but the investment pays tremendous dividends over time. Boundaries create the space necessary for your priorities to flourish. Without them, external demands and distractions can consistently derail your progress. They are the guidelines you establish to protect what matters most in your life. They define what you will and will not accept in terms of how you spend your time, energy, and attention. These limits create clear separations between your priorities and the endless demands that compete for your resources. They include the restrictions you set with others and limitations you establish for yourself.

Enforcing personal rules with others can often require tremendous courage, yet it can also provide exponential benefits. Having direct, honest conversations with people who consistently create drama or negativity in your life protects your mental state. Establishing clear ground rules about how you will accept being treated by others becomes essential. This includes family members, friends, romantic partners, business colleagues, and everyone in between. Learning when to engage in crucial conversations and when to disengage entirely, including how much to distance yourself from relationships that drain your energy rather than support your growth, is a critical life skill.

Setting digital boundaries also proves essential in our connected world. Limiting social media exposure helps negate constant interruptions and decreases exposure to negative feedback. Reducing consumption of negative news prevents mental energy from being drained by information you cannot control. Setting specific hours for checking and responding to phone calls, text messages, emails, or other various forms of electronic correspondences creates more focused work periods without frequent notification anxiety or decreased momentum from other important tasks.

Another area of importance is learning to decline commitments that do not align with your priorities, as it further prevents overcommitment and burnout. Beyond creating external boundaries, self-imposed boundaries can be equally transformative. This includes establishing limits around your own behaviors, which demonstrates self-respect and reinforces commitments to positive change. This might involve refraining from consuming foods or substances that leave you feeling sluggish or abstaining from activities that undermine your aspirations. It also encompasses what we have already discussed: protecting calendar time through strategic scheduling, establishing consistent habits, and reducing any negativity from your life that drains your focus and energy.

The last reinforcement practice, social influences, is the impact that other people have on your mindset, decisions, and actions through their words, behaviors, and energy. The people we spend time with significantly influence our thoughts, behaviors, and long-term outcomes. While we cannot control others' actions, we can certainly control our own by being intentional about our social environment. This involves both removing negative influences and actively seeking positive ones. Distancing yourself from individuals who consistently discredit your aspirations or feed into your limiting beliefs protects the mindset work you have been developing. Simultaneously, connecting with people who share your values and ambitions creates natural accountability and inspiration. Seeking coaches, mentors, accountability partners, or growth-focused communities reinforces the positive thought patterns and behaviors that drive achievement. These relationships provide encouragement during challenging periods and celebrate progress along the way.

These foundational principles are part of why we taught you about "*The 3-4-30 Challenge*SM" and the practices of mindset reinforcement, and these work most effectively when implemented together. "*The 3-4-30 Challenge*SM" enables you to integrate all four elements together. Strategically scheduling your challenge actions over thirty-day timelines ensures consistent progress through non-negotiable calendar commitments. These planned actions develop into routines that create habits, causing beneficial behaviors to become increasingly more automatic. Successfully completing "*The 3-4-30 Challenge*SM" typically requires enforcing boundaries that protect your focus from competing demands. The ongoing accountability and support inherent in every challenge participation promotes positive social influences that maintain motivation and dedication. The beauty of this approach extends far beyond achieving individual aspirations. Each challenge builds the underlying systems and patterns that make future achievements far more attainable.

Most people think about what they want without restructuring their environment, calendar, and relationships to support their desires. When you align your schedule, routines, boundaries, and social influences with your aspirations and actions, positive outcomes become more of a byproduct rather than a constant battle.

The combination of mindset reinforcement and structured implementation separates those who struggle from those who consistently attain their desires. You now understand how to train your mind for growth and organize your life for intentional execution. However, one final element determines long-term success: the power of consistency. Getting started is one thing, but sustaining progress requires a repeatable process that promotes continuous improvement. This is exactly what we will explore in the next chapter as we discuss how to further track progress, adjust course when necessary, and maintain momentum over the long term.

These implementation practices require deeper exploration than we can provide here. Our *Tilting The Balance*™: *A Guided Workbook for Clarity, Purpose, and Transformation* offers more comprehensive guidance on habit psychology, schedule optimization, and boundary-setting without guilt or resistance. As always, for personalized support in implementing any of these practices, our coaching services offer direct support and ongoing accountability.

You can obtain your copy of our workbook at www.TiltingTheBalance.com/BuyNow or learn more about our available coaching services by visiting www.TiltingTheBalance.com/LiveLearning.

CHAPTER 7:
THE POWER OF CONSISTENCY: HOW TO STAY ON TRACK & KEEP GROWING

Consistency is what separates those who achieve fulfillment and results from those who remain stuck in cycles of unhappiness and uncertainty. It is not about relying solely on willpower, as true perseverance stems from purpose. When you have a strong reason behind your actions, clarity, focus, and motivation naturally emerge to sustain commitment. Purpose, paired with dedication, builds discipline, which reinforces lasting habits and ultimately drives results.

Many people believe success is about intensity, but that is often a mistake. To create real lasting change usually requires steady effort over time. While pushing hard for short periods can create traction, failing to pace yourself over extended periods generally leads to burnout. Physical, mental, emotional, and spiritual exhaustion can be a massive detriment to your overall well-being. Therefore, we advise gradually repeating smaller, intentional actions, as they tend to be more manageable while helping to preserve precious energy. This approach can also drive greater long-term results than shorter bursts of extreme effort. As we reviewed prior, this occurs because repeated behaviors strengthen neural pathways, forming habits that make future actions more automatic. The true key to optimal sustainability and lasting results is balance, which is the foundation of the entire *Tilting The Balance*™ system.

Showing up regularly reinforces confidence. When you repeatedly follow through on commitments, it trains you to better trust in yourself. Progress does not always look the same each day, but what matters is that you continue to show up. Some days may bring major breakthroughs, while others might seem uneventful, but it is your collective efforts that yield results. A phenomenal way to maintain momentum is to create and appreciate small, daily wins. Simple habits, like making your bed every morning, set the tone for accomplishment. They can reinforce the identity that you are someone who is capable and reliable.

The little things often have the greatest compounding effects that usually extend far beyond what is immediately visible. Eating a slice of cake in a single serving may not tremendously impact your overall health, but eating one every day over time can definitely lead to negative consequences. An individual workout by itself is unlikely to drastically transform your body, but following a regular exercise routine week over week most certainly can. This principle applies to the majority of your habits. Remember, since it can be easy to become overwhelmed by substantial goals, starting small tricks the mind into seeing change as manageable. Beginning with an emphasis on more minimal objectives removes resistance, builds that momentum, and allows your desired outcomes to better follow as a result.

It is important to understand what is defined as overall success. If a target is set and actualized, success has occurred. If a goal is set and does not become achieved, success has again occurred, but this time in the form of obtaining optimization data. That information reveals which aspects of your approach worked, which ones did not, and where pivoting may become most necessary. The biggest mistake people make is dwelling on perceived setbacks as failures rather than using them as positive feedback. John C. Maxwell wrote a best-selling book, *Sometimes You Win, Sometimes You Learn*, and that title, in itself, reveals the reality of progress. Every time something does not go as planned, an opportunity emerges to adjust, recalibrate, and move forward with empowering insight. When one door closes, another opens, and the possibilities that follow can exceed anything you may have previously imagined. As the authors of *Tilting The Balance*™, we can both speak to that. Sometimes things do not transpire based on our personal preferences because something far greater is already on its way. Maintaining gratitude for all of your current blessings in these instances can help keep up the needed momentum until new opportunities arise.

This philosophy extends to handling restarts. Many people become paralyzed by their pasts, allowing guilt or fear to dictate their current and future actions. They beat themselves up for needing to start over or take a new approach, rather than seeing circumstances as a natural part of the process. *Waking the Tiger* by Peter Levine explains how animals do not hold onto trauma the way humans do. A deer that escapes a predator cannot, and generally does not, remain frozen in fear. Instead, it shakes off the situation and continues on. It must. Otherwise, if it stops, it can become an easy meal for the next predator that comes along.

For humans, however, due to our high levels of conscious awareness, we can allow our past memories to replay repeatedly in our minds. This can let difficult emotions persist and affect our well-being over time, causing negative feelings associated with the past to perpetuate into our futures. To further support breaking free of these cycles, we must proceed without judgment while working toward releasing unhelpful viewpoints of the past, reducing anxious anticipation of the future, and mastering the art of staying present. While these are valuable practices, it is important to acknowledge that healing from significant trauma often requires professional support and cannot simply be willed away. The mission is progress, not perfection, and everyone's healing journey unfolds at its own pace.

As long as we have time on this earth, restarts allow us the opportunity for new beginnings. Obstacles, setbacks, and failures are merely narratives surrounding our circumstances, and can serve as nothing more than lessons in disguise. Our experiences, guided by our perceptions, are simply what we label them to be. We must learn not to resist the natural ebbs and flows of life, and to control our outlook when things do not go exactly as planned. Expect the unexpected, learn from your mistakes, and let go of the past along with all the things in life that no longer positively serve you. Keep your sights on what means the most to you and enjoy every step of the journey along the way. There are no real failures in life unless you stop learning, growing, and putting in the effort entirely.

Every challenge is feedback. Every restart is an opportunity to refine your approach and succeed again. Quitting too soon can cost you everything. The Napoleon Hill Foundation, along with Greg Reid and Sharon Lechter, published the book, *Three Feet from Gold*, which tells the story of R.U. Darby, a man who borrowed money from family and friends to invest in a gold mine during the Colorado gold rush era. After an initial exciting discovery of gold, and a tremendous amount of time spent searching, the vein they struck miraculously vanished. After continuing to search to no avail, he and his partners gave up, selling the mine to a local junk man for only a few hundred dollars.

What they did not know was that they had stopped digging just three feet away from one of the richest gold deposits ever found in the region. Because the junk man was wise enough to have sought expert counsel, he ended up making millions, and although Darby lost out on the mine, he learned a powerful lesson about persistence and about the value of seeking expert guidance. The story had a happy ending, as Darby later repaid his debts and achieved great success in the insurance business.

Some of the most prominent people in history have experienced countless setbacks before reaching greatness. When creating the lightbulb, Thomas Edison famously said, "I have not failed. I have just found ten thousand ways that do not work." Michael Jordan was cut from his high school basketball team before becoming one of the greatest athletes in NBA history. Walt Disney was fired from a newspaper job for "lacking creativity" before he built an entertainment empire. J.K. Rowling faced numerous rejections from publishers before her Harry Potter saga became a global phenomenon. Suzy Batiz went bankrupt twice before launching Poo-Pourri, which grew into a multimillion-dollar brand. The common thread among them all? Not a single one allowed themselves to be discouraged by the judgment of others or let anything that could have been perceived as a failure define them. Instead, they learned, adapted, and kept going with relentless determination.

To further solidify the point, not everyone who has achieved greatness has done so in the field they originally envisioned themselves in. Samuel Morse, trained as a painter in Europe and known for his portraits, invented Morse code after his wife died before he could reach her in time. Her passing drove him to develop a system that would speed up communication so others would not share in the same devastating delay. Samuel Adams, one of America's Founding Fathers, was called a "poor businessman" by his own father after his established brewery failed. The irony? A popular beer brand carries his name today. Colonel Sanders did not start Kentucky Fried Chicken until he was sixty-two years old, after numerous failed ventures. Vera Wang entered the fashion industry and became an iconic name in bridal gowns after careers in figure skating and journalism. These stories remind us that our dreams can evolve, directions can change, and success can still materialize in the most unexpected ways.

Even for us as the authors of *Tilting The Balance*™, our journeys took unexpected turns. Nick originally sought to become a police officer before becoming involved in senior care, and Justin switched from the insurance business to pursue building a real estate enterprise, until we both realized how much we wanted to impact others through this transformative work. Sometimes the greatest achievements emerge not from following the original plan, but from remaining open to where life leads. The willingness to pivot, to embrace new opportunities, and to trust in the process along the way can reveal outcomes far beyond what we ever could have imagined possible.

When you can master the art of moving forward positively, appreciating the present moments as much as possible, while embracing the fact that every moment can set the stage for something even greater, the more unstoppable you can become. No matter where you currently are or how you feel about yourself, choosing to step into any meaningful role always comes with a level of uncertainty. Things will not always go as planned, nor will they always unfold as expected. That is still not a valid reason to hesitate. If anything, it is more of a reason to act regardless. Keeping all of this in the forefront of your mind, you must have the courage to start, and once you do, the merit to continue on.

Another dynamic to appreciate is the evergreen balance between timing and opportunity. There are many occasions where time must unfold before the best opportunities can materialize. In other instances, fantastic options may present themselves at the most inopportune moments. It can be difficult to remember this when particular situations occur that may not go exactly as desired, yet the reality is that hindsight usually reveals how they transpired for a purpose. What the purpose ends up being, though, depends entirely on your perspective, your ability to persevere through adversity with a positive mindset, and the great mystery of life and what it might present next.

The truth is, no one has all the answers. No one can predict exactly how every event will pan out. If we could, it might seem like life would be easier, but would it? Imagine if we knew everything that was about to happen. At first, this idea might sound like a relief, but in the real world, it would more likely become its own burden. The uncertainty we fear now could very well be replaced with the paralysis of knowing. Instead of stepping forward with confidence in some cases, the terror of taking action could emerge. Not knowing is part of the gift of life. It gives us the freedom to try, to grow, to adapt, and to embrace the adventures of life without being weighed down by the fear of a predetermined outcome.

This is how visionary practices such as the Chief Aim Statement serve as a foundation for long-term dedication. While discipline can keep someone on track, a clear vision maintains inspiration. Without a strong connection to long-term missions, it is easier to get caught up in the day-to-day and lose sight of why we started in the first place. Some other effective ways to maintain this connection include crafting the mission and vision statements we referred to earlier in the book. These statements act as an internal compass, guiding decisions, reinforcing values, and maintaining focus on priorities. These are not just motivational phrases. They are declarations of who you are and who you further intend to become, both personally and professionally. For detailed guidance on how to structure these powerful statements for yourself, visit www.TiltingTheBalance.com/Statements.

Another impactful tool is the dream board, also known as a vision board. Creating a visual representation of your goals already being accomplished engages the subconscious mind, making success feel more real and achievable. Studies have shown that the brain does not differentiate between vividly imagined experiences and reality. The more deeply you can see the outcomes of yourself having achieved the objects of your desires, the more likely you are to take decisive actions and experience realities that are in alignment with those visions.

Beyond these resources is another transformative practice that we call Vision Gazing^{SM}. This takes visualization to a deeper level where success is not only pictured but felt through full immersion in the emotions and sensory associations of already having achieved it. This practice allows complete embodiment of the future reality so that the mind begins to treat success as an expectation rather than a potential possibility.

What makes these visionary practices so effective is that they can transform steady commitments from obligations into aspects of your identity. When seeing oneself as someone who follows through, takes initiative, and remains dedicated, that new identity evolves into a self-fulfilling prophecy. Forcing yourself to take action no longer becomes necessary. It becomes second nature.

In the end, it is not about perfection. It is about showing up, doing your best, and staying in alignment with your long-term desires. That is how these visionary practices, combined with ongoing implementation, can aid in persevering further toward success.

If we can help support you in any way, please know that our lives are dedicated to helping others be at their best. Our dreams come true when yours do. Visit www.TiltingTheBalance.com/LiveLearning to explore our coaching services and learn how we can be a direct resource for you along your personal development journey.

CONCLUSION

Congratulations! By reaching this point, you have already achieved a significant accomplishment. You have officially read a book! You are also now equipped with all of the basics needed to begin experiencing life-changing results right away. Every great transformation begins with a single step. Just like how interest accumulates on an investment, the effort you put in today can multiply in ways you cannot yet see. What may feel like small shifts now could be setting the foundation for opportunities far greater than you might have ever expected. It all begins with implementing the strategies we have reviewed together.

Think back to where you were when you first picked up this book. Maybe you felt stuck, frustrated, or overwhelmed. Maybe you had a vision of success but struggled to follow through, unsure of how to bridge the gap between where you were and where you wanted to be. Perhaps you had tried countless strategies before, only to fall into the same patterns, wondering why nothing seemed to work.

Now, take a moment to reflect on what has changed since you started this journey with us. You have learned of the power in quieting distractions, releasing the weight of past regrets, and freeing yourself from anxieties about the future. By embracing the magnetic energy of the present, you now have the ability to focus on what matters most. You have learned how to gain clarity on your goals and aspirations by organizing your thoughts with "The Mind Dump" exercise and about how to live with more purpose by defining your Ikigai, along with your mission, vision, and Chief Aim Statements. You are also empowered with the understanding that utilizing further visionary practices such as creating dream boards and engaging in Vision Gazing^SM can provide long-term motivation, reinforcing belief in what is possible. You understand the value of reinforcing your mindset through powerful practices such as affirmations, visualization, meditation, and gratitude, and know the importance of training your mind to align with success rather than self-doubt.

You also know how to implement a structured approach to execution, understanding the power of hard scheduling, routines, and boundaries to ensure that your time and energy are spent on what actually moves progress forward. Lastly, you have been introduced to "*The 3-4-30 Challenge^SM*," the ultimate implementation system designed to create accountability and progress that you can begin using right away to apply everything we have reviewed. All of these discoveries reinforce that real progress does not come from total intensity but from steady, purpose-driven, intentional actions repeated over time.

While there is always much more in life to learn, you now have a clear, repeatable system designed to eliminate uncertainty, replace inconsistency with momentum, and change self-doubt into courage and self-confidence. With these approaches working together systemically, you are no longer navigating in the dark. The truth is, however, that knowledge alone does not create results. Only action can turn ideas into reality. Real transformation begins the moment you decide to routinely implement these practices into your daily activities.

Tilting The Balance™ is the very system that transformed our lives in ways we never imagined when we first began. Before we discovered these principles, we struggled with many of the same challenges most people face. We set goals but lacked the structure to follow through. We had big dreams but allowed distractions, setbacks, coping mechanisms, and self-doubt to slow us down. Everything changed when we realized that success is not about working harder or chasing motivation. It is about working smarter by following a repeatable process that brings our ideas to life.

That is exactly how *Tilting The Balance*™ was born. We started by working to best help ourselves, and after spending over half a decade to refine our individual approaches, we realized that its power can help anyone who is willing to help themselves.

The impact behind *Tilting The Balance*™ is reflected in the lives of others who have worked with us, experiencing life-changing results of their own. Here is what others who have worked directly with us and utilized our system have had to say:

"Coach Justin has been not only a mentor and motivator, but helped with setting goals and figuring out the steps I need to take to reach them. He proved that he could understand my niche type of business and gave me the confidence I needed to finally get my business off the ground."
– Daniel D.

"A good coach always listens and tells you the truth and then tells you how to solve it. Nick uses love over judgment, and I always call or text him with all of my life questions."
– Jesse J.

"Justin is one of those very special people you only meet a few times in life. When we first started working together I quickly discovered an immediate spark that he possesses. The gameplan, accountability and overall organization I got from Coach Justin Bullock was absolutely unmatched. I'd give 1000 stars if I could. Thanks, Justin!"
– Adam L.

"One of the things I appreciate most about Nick is his ability to give sound advice. He does not just tell you what you want to hear. He tells you what you need to hear. His advice is always practical, realistic, and tailored to your specific situation."
– Amanda W.

We are beyond appreciative for their kind words from those we have assisted and are always grateful to have the opportunity to help anyone become their best selves or reach their greatest dreams. We believe everyone has the power to do so.

The greatest achievers, from athletes to entrepreneurs, have proven that success is not about natural talent alone. They show up, put in the work, and commit to the process even when results are not immediate. These are the direct choices that led them to success. The same is true for you. The difference between where you are now and where you want to be is your willingness to remain consistent in working to be your best self. This is your opportunity to commit.

The path to personal and professional mastery is now in front of you, and the next phase of your personal growth comes from fully integrating this systematic approach into your life. We strongly encourage you to continue your journey from here with *Tilting The Balance*™: *A Guided Workbook for Clarity, Purpose, and Transformation*. Introducing "The 10 Categories of Life," this resource has been specifically designed to help you implement the practices introduced in this book in a much more structured, step-by-step way. While the book you have just read certainly provides all of the insights you need to get started, the workbook equips you with further tools to create meaningful change and lasting results. It expands upon every major concept covered here and explores a wide range of additional techniques and practical strategies that are essential for lasting success.

If you are ready to go all in to use this system to reach your greatest heights, *Tilting The Balance*™: *A Guided Workbook for Clarity, Purpose, and Transformation* is available at www.TiltingTheBalance.com/BuyNow.

As we mentioned, you also do not have to figure everything out solely on your own. We offer direct, expert guidance to help you incorporate these principles into your life with full support, structured accountability, and personalized mentorship. You may choose to work with us either one-on-one or in a group coaching setting. If you would like to explore these options further, visit www.TiltingTheBalance.com/LiveLearning.

As the authors, we both thank you so much for taking the time to read our work. We are grateful for all of your time and hope you have found all of our insights to be informative and impactful. You should now have everything you need to start creating the life you want most. The only remaining question is, are you ready to make it happen?

ABOUT COACH JUSTIN BULLOCK

A Florida native, originally from Tallahassee, Justin grew up in a hardworking, entrepreneurial family that instilled in him the values of perseverance and ambition. His adoptive father's advice, "Success is having balance in all areas of your life," sparked a mindset shift that continues to guide his mission today.

From an early age, he demonstrated an entrepreneurial spirit. He washed cars in his neighborhood (primarily to fund his early love of junk food) and worked full-time physical labor jobs during his high school summers to earn extra income, including roles as a land surveyor, landscaper, and roofer. These early experiences, paired with the mentorship of key figures throughout his life, shaped his values for appreciating hard work.

After moving to Jacksonville, Florida to pursue a career as a health insurance broker, a wrongful termination combined with a chance encounter with a potential customer led Justin to a life-changing mentorship. Under his mentor's guidance, he became immersed in learning about real estate and how to operate e-commerce businesses, discovering a passion that would redefine his entire personal and professional trajectory.

Shortly after becoming a licensed Realtor® in 2016, Justin founded and operated multiple real estate and construction companies within five years, raised millions in capital for real estate investment syndications and small business funding, and successfully sold and managed several hundred collective real estate and construction transactions. However, his greatest lessons came not from victories alone, but from perceived challenges, failures, and setbacks that revealed the need for a system to better navigate life with purpose and understanding. This realization became the catalyst for developing the *Tilting The Balance*™ framework alongside Nick.

After years of building those businesses, Justin made a pivotal decision to close his companies and commit fully to his true calling of coaching and further developing *Tilting The Balance*™. While he maintains his real estate license and continues to serve select individuals, his primary focus has shifted to helping others create extraordinary lives through the principles that had transformed his own. This strategic shift from building traditional businesses to empowering others reflected his deepening commitment to making a meaningful impact through his entrepreneurial expertise and life experience.

With extensive coaching certifications including designations as a Master Life Coach, Master Health and Wellness Coach, Master Mindset Coach, and Entrepreneurship & Business Coach, paired with his own personal experiences, Justin brings deep expertise in life mastery, business, relationships, and wellness. He strives to help individuals gain clarity, build confidence, and take meaningful action across all areas of life.

Justin specializes in supporting career growth, financial literacy, book writing, and real estate investing, providing structured pathways for professional advancement. His guidance extends to establishing purpose, mastering goal setting, time management, and helping those who struggle with planning or procrastination to develop lasting commitments that keep them motivated, accountable, and taking aligned action. For those seeking deeper romantic connections, his relationship coaching offers insights on how to spark and maintain attraction, communicate effectively, and develop greater emotional intelligence that impacts all life areas. Whether someone needs to optimize their mindset, elevate their professional and financial life, strengthen their relationships, or enhance their overall quality of life, Justin is passionate about providing clarity, structure, and a proven path forward.

Beyond his coaching and business operations, Justin channels his creativity through multiple musical ventures. He co-founded *Affirmation Station Music*, an innovative project that transforms the music landscape by embedding science-backed affirmations into emotionally moving songs across all genres. This unique approach combines intentional language with captivating sound, creating music that uplifts, heals, and rewires the subconscious mind with empowering beliefs. Justin also writes and performs original works under the name *Woodland Drives*, serves as lead singer and guitarist in a local cover band, and even teaches basic guitar fundamentals through his course *Memorize The Guitar*. Having played music since the age of six, it remains an integral part of his life. He plans to release more albums and help others grow in the music industry while continuing to inspire through creativity and connection.

Have a question or a comment directly for Coach Justin? Visit TiltingTheBalance.com/ContactUs to send a message today.

ABOUT COACH NICOLAS HOUPT

What started as a personal journey to find balance, healing, and fulfillment has become a mission to help others live with intention and clarity.

Nicolas Houpt is an author, speaker, and mental health advocate who helps people reconnect with what matters most, within themselves and in the world around them. His work is built on the one core belief that you do not have to do it all to live a life that feels whole; you just have to do what promotes optimal meaning and fulfillment, with a clear mind and a steady heart. He reminds us that balance is not about doing everything. It is about doing the right things, with presence, love, and a grounded sense of who we are.

Raised in Pittsburgh, Nick's entrepreneurial spirit sparked early. From selling bubble gum at the age of twelve to building a network marketing organization in his early twenties, he understood the value of hard work and opportunity. However, it was not until years later, through seasons of burnout, toxic patterns with alcohol, and personal struggle, that Nick began to redefine what success actually meant. He realized that financial gain and status alone were not the goal, but rather, genuine happiness, meaningful connection, and self-awareness. but rather, genuine happiness, meaningful connection, and self-awareness. That awakening shifted everything.

As he began applying the principles that would later become the foundation for *Tilting The Balance*™, Nick broke free from destructive habits, reshaped his mindset, and started living with greater clarity, discipline, and purpose. His own transformation, fueled by small, intentional choices, proved that lasting change is not about perfection but consistent progress and impact.

Today, Nick works in the mental health field and hosts the Life Well Balanced Podcast, where he leads genuine conversations about balance, presence, and mental wellness. Whether on stage, in an interview, or face-to-face, Nick speaks from a place of authenticity, sharing his story to help inspire others to more positively write theirs.

A devoted husband and father, he is committed to living the message he shares. Through his writing, speaking, and everyday life, he encourages others to create space for what they deem to be most important, to slow down long enough to enjoy themselves along the way, and to step into the life they were meant to live.

www.ingramcontent.com/pod-product-compliance
Lightning Source LLC
Chambersburg PA
CBHW051556120626
46551CB00013B/1544